WHaT
SiZE
iS
iT?

Charles Hatcher

drawings by
Gareth Adamson

Duell, Sloan and Pearce   New York

THUMBS, HANDS

ONE YARD

ONE INCH

ONE FOOT

Let's begin with a riddle:

Why is a man's body like a ruler?

Because a long time ago, before rulers were invented, various parts of the body were used to measure the size of things.

An *inch* was the width of a man's thumb.

A *foot* was simply the length, from heel to big toe, of a man's foot!

A *yard* was the distance from a man's nose to the tips of his fingers when his arm was stretched out straight in front of him.

Although these *units of measurement* were very useful, they caused a lot of trouble at times.

A big man's yard was smaller than a small man's, so if he went to buy something by the yard, like cloth, he got more than a small man did.

And if a mother sent her child shopping for a yard or a foot of something like ribbon or paper, she would get less than if she went herself, because the child's arm or foot was smaller than hers.

HIS

HERS

& ATOMS

BRITISH STANDARD YARD

Pure gold   *Pure gold*

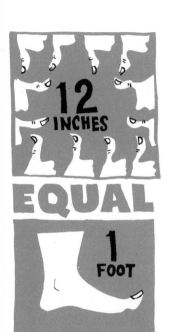

12 INCHES

EQUAL

1 FOOT

There were many arguments among merchants and shopkeepers, which often led to fights.

It was finally decided to fix a standard inch, foot and yard, making them the same for everybody to use.

Twelve inches was to be equal to one foot, and three feet to one yard.

Today a *standard yard* is kept in a vault in London.

It is a bar of the precious metal *platinum*. Set into the ends of the bar are plugs of pure gold. A mark is engraved on each plug. The distance between the two engraved marks is exactly one *yard*.

All yardsticks, foot rules and measuring tapes used by merchants, storekeepers, engineers and architects must be the same as the standard yard.

Other units of length are used for special purposes.

The width of a man's hand is used to measure the height of a horse. Horses are measured in *hands!*

3 FEET

EQUAL

1 YARD

171726

4

Sailors measure the depths of the oceans in *fathoms*.

A fathom was invented from the size of a man's body. It was the distance between the tips of his fingers when both his arms were stretched out sideways.

Today a fathom is equal to *six feet*, or twice the length of the standard yard kept in London.

Sailors didn't dive into the sea to make depth measurements, however! They simply measured a long rope with their outstretched arms, tied knots in it at fathom intervals, and then used a heavy weight to lower their measuring rope into the sea.

But today scientists who study the depths of the oceans generally use feet instead of fathoms. Did you know that some parts of the Pacific Ocean are more than 30,000 feet deep? No ship in the old days could have carried enough knotted rope to measure such a depth in fathoms!

ONE FATHOM

SAUCY L

To find the Metric equivalent of inches(or vice-versa hold a straight-edged paper across the

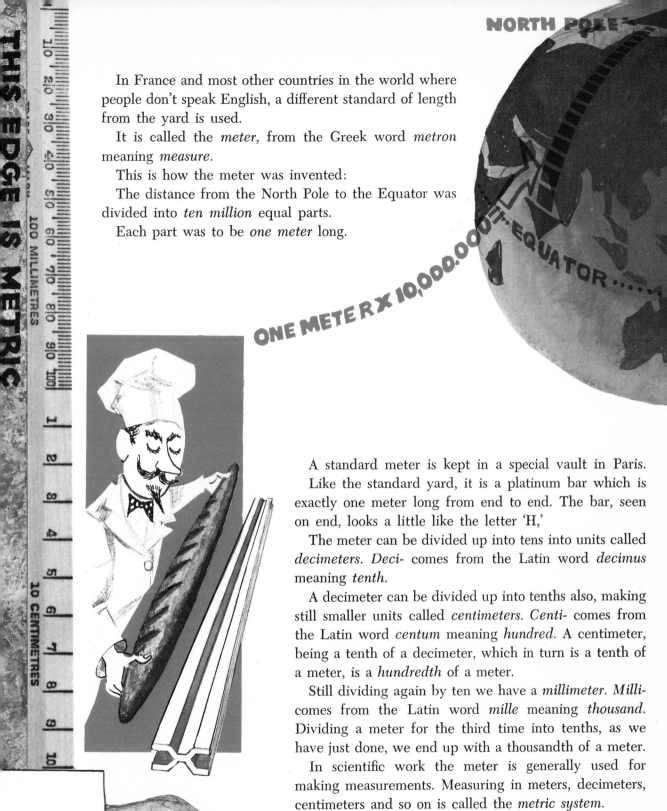

THIS EDGE IS METRIC

In France and most other countries in the world where people don't speak English, a different standard of length from the yard is used.

It is called the *meter*, from the Greek word *metron* meaning *measure*.

This is how the meter was invented:

The distance from the North Pole to the Equator was divided into *ten million* equal parts.

Each part was to be *one meter* long.

ONE METER X 10,000,000

EQUATOR

A standard meter is kept in a special vault in Paris.

Like the standard yard, it is a platinum bar which is exactly one meter long from end to end. The bar, seen on end, looks a little like the letter 'H,'

The meter can be divided up into tens into units called *decimeters*. Deci- comes from the Latin word *decimus* meaning *tenth*.

A decimeter can be divided up into tenths also, making still smaller units called *centimeters*. Centi- comes from the Latin word *centum* meaning *hundred*. A centimeter, being a tenth of a decimeter, which in turn is a tenth of a meter, is a *hundredth* of a meter.

Still dividing again by ten we have a *millimeter*. Milli- comes from the Latin word *mille* meaning *thousand*. Dividing a meter for the third time into tenths, as we have just done, we end up with a thousandth of a meter.

In scientific work the meter is generally used for making measurements. Measuring in meters, decimeters, centimeters and so on is called the *metric system*.

This astronaut, travelling at speeds of thousands of miles an hour in his space capsule, needs special units of measurement.

One of these is called *Mach*, which is the number of times he travels faster than the speed of sound.

At Mach One he travels at the speed of sound, or 740 miles per hour, which is not very fast for an astronaut.

At Mach Two he travels at twice the speed of sound or 1,480 miles per hour, which is the speed of a modern jet fighter.

At Mach Twenty he would be travelling at 14,800 miles an hour, which is just about right for an astronaut in orbit!

Ernst Mach, by the way, was a famous German scientist who first measured the speed of sound waves caused when a gun was fired. So his name was given to this special high-speed measurement.

93 MILLION MILES

Modern astronomers use a *very* long unit of measurement, which they call *Astronomical Unit* or AU for short.

An AU is 93,000,000 miles, which is the average distance between the Earth and the Sun.

Astronomers have been able to measure quite accurately stars which are more than a million million AU's away, which is more than 93 million million *million* miles! These stars, of course, can only be seen with our most powerful telescopes.

The smallest unit of all is called a *Fermi,* invented by the famous atomic scientist Enrico Fermi. It is used to measure things as tiny as molecules and even atoms.

A Fermi is equal to the distance across a *proton*, one of the incredibly tiny particles inside the *nucleus* or "core" of an atom.

A Fermi is about one twenty-million-*millionth* of an inch!

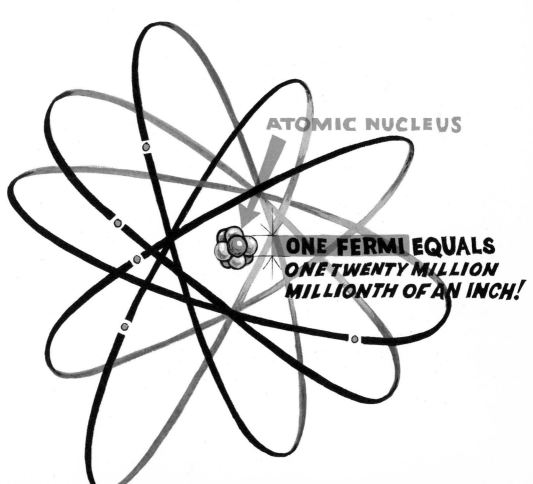

ATOMIC NUCLEUS

ONE FERMI EQUALS ONE TWENTY MILLION MILLIONTH OF AN INCH!

It's easy to measure the lengths of *straight* things like platinum bars, the edges of tables and boxes.

But measuring the lengths of curving edges of saucepans, the shores of treasure islands and the twisting path you take through a wood is much more difficult.

If you found yourself on a desert island you *could* walk all the way round it, measuring little bits of the shore with a ruler. Then you could simply add all your measurements together, probably thousands of them!

And your total measurement wouldn't be very accurate.

Draw a fairly large circle with a compass. Then make a mark on the edge (called the *circumference* of the circle) and start measuring the whole circumference in little bits with one of the quarter-inch divisions on a ruler.

Make a mark each time you measure a quarter of an inch.

Add up all your measurements.

Now draw the same circle again, and ask a friend to measure the circumference in the same way. You'll be surprised how different his total measurement will be from yours!

Doubloon Bay
• Morganstown
• Crossbones Castle
Cutlass
Dead Man's Reach
• Kyddshaven
Wreckers • Run
Rat-trap Bay

Here is a simple machine you can make for measuring curves and circles and the shores of countries on maps.

Draw a circle on a piece of stiff card which has a *radius* (distance from the *center* to anywhere on the *circumference*) of just under half an inch.

Do this by placing the point of the compass on the 'zero' mark of your ruler and setting the point of the pencil just between the half-inch mark and the sixteenth-inch mark below it. The circle you have drawn will have a circumference of *just about three inches.*

Cut out the circle and make a small pencil mark anywhere on the circumference. Fix the circle to a stick of wood by pushing a drawing pin through the center. Make sure the circle turns freely. The best length for the stick is about six or seven inches.

The machine you have made is called an *opisometer* which comes from two Greek words and means "measuring backwards."

Here is how you use it:

Place the edge of the circle on any curving line you want to measure, such as the shore on a large map or a wavy chalk line drawn on the pavement.

Turn the circle until the circumference mark you made is next to the line.

Now carefully run your opisometer along the line, following it as the circle turns. The more carefully you steer your machine, the more accurate your measurement will be.

Count the number of times the circle turns. Each time the mark leaves the line and then comes back to it your circle has turned once and you have measured *three inches* of the line.

The total number of turns your wheel made *multiplied* by three gives you the total length of the curving line in inches.

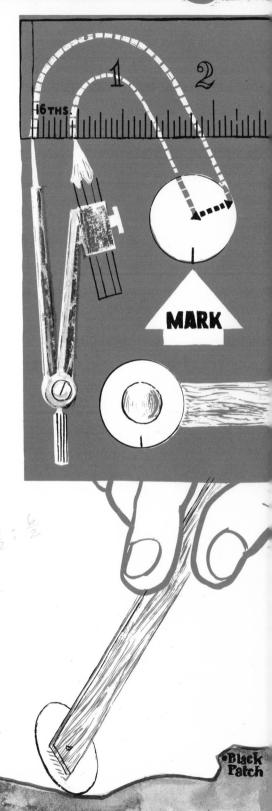

Hooks Point

Rum Cove

Skeleton Quay

Yoho Hoe

Black Patch

You can make a much bigger opisometer to measure how far you can walk when you go from your front door to a nearby shop or to your school. Simply use a much longer stick. A broom handle will do nicely.

Make a much bigger circle, using heavier cardboard. This time set your compass just under one and seven-eighths inches. This will give you a circle on the card with a circumference of *one foot*.

Make a clear pencil mark on the circumference as you did when you made your smaller machine.

It's better to use a large carpet tack or a short nail rather than a drawing pin.

Make sure that the tack or nail is driven in tightly enough for your circle not to wobble, yet not so tightly that it won't turn freely.

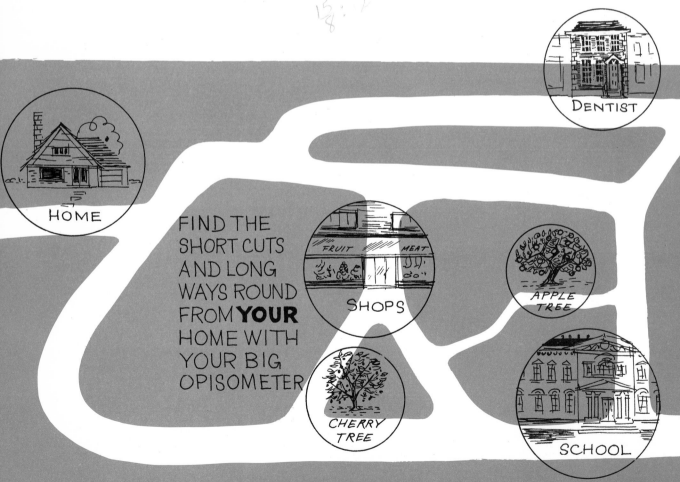

TRY YOUR LITTLE OPISOMETER ON THIS MAP

MILEAGE INDICATOR
IS USUALLY HERE

YES, THAT'S
THE HORN—
*LEAVE IT
ALONE!*

The mileage indicator on the instrument panel of an automobile works in the same way as your opisometers.

A special mechanism inside the car simply *counts* the number of times the wheels of the car turn. This mechanism then works the little numbers you can see in the window of the indicator.

You can also use your large opisometer to find out how fast you walk.

First make a chalk mark on the pavement. Then walk along with your opisometer until it has turned its circle 100 times.

Then stop and make another chalk mark on the pavement.

The distance between the two chalk marks is 100 feet.

Now ask a friend to use the second hand of his watch to time how long it takes you to walk from one mark to the other.

Simply *divide* the number of seconds he counted with his watch into 100, which is the distance in feet you have walked. The result is your walking speed, in *feet* per *second*.

100 ÷ seconds = feet per second walking speed.

Radar is used today to measure the distance away of things that can't be reached with tape measures.

Radar has been used to measure how far away the Moon is. This is how radar works:

Imagine that you could travel all the way to the Moon in a spaceship, without stopping or slowing down.

By using a clock to time how long your journey took, and knowing at what speed in miles per hour your ship travelled during the whole journey, you could easily calculate the Moon's distance from the Earth.

Radar works in the same way, except that the radar antenna, a big bowl of steel, sends a *radio signal* to the Moon. The radio signal reaches the Moon and then bounces back, all the way to the radar antenna again.

Complicated electronic "brains" or computers inside the radar station calculate how long the "radio" journey has taken.

And we know how fast radio waves travel—186,000 miles per second.

So the radar's electronic computer makes the same kind of calculation as we did in our spaceship to find the Moon's distance away from the Earth.

Architects and builders use *tapes* to make measurements.

Imagine measuring the length of your living room with a ruler. It would have to hop across the floor many times. And your measurements wouldn't be very accurate.

THIS IS A SILLY WAY TO MEASURE A FLOOR...

MAKE A TAPE MEASURE!

You can make a tape measure with a piece of white string about twenty feet long. Use a ruler to mark it up into feet and inches with crayons. Mark every foot with a red crayon. Mark every inch with a blue or black crayon.

Use your tape measure to find out the lengths and widths of the rooms in your flat or house.

Then make an architect's plan of your home like the one shown on the opposite page.

To do this you will need a *scale*.

For every distance of *one foot* you measure, you draw a line *a quarter of an inch* long on your plan.

Suppose a room is sixteen feet wide when you measure it. Then the distance you make on your plan should be *four* inches.

To help you we have drawn a scale on the plan.

Notice that each foot distance has been conveniently divided up into *halves* and *quarters* of a foot. In making your room measurements, make them to the nearest half or quarter of a foot. This will help you to make a simpler plan.

Architect's plans look exactly like this. They are called *blueprints*.

BEDROOM

BEDROOM

STAIRS
DOWN

BATH-
ROOM

BEDROOM

SCALE-QUARTER INCH EQUALS ONE FOOT

Astronomers, too, use scales to make measurements. On the opposite page is an astronomer's photograph of the Moon. Its *diameter* (distance across) is 2,160 miles.

We have used this distance as a scale, which is the line drawn next to the Moon's diameter. The small divisions from 0 to 100 are twenty miles each. The large divisions are one hundred miles each.

You can use this photograph and the scale to measure for yourself the diameters of some of the famous craters on the Moon.

Place the edge of a piece of paper across the widest part of the crater you wish to measure and make two marks where the rim of the crater meets the paper's edge.

Then place the edge of the paper against the scale. One of the marks you've made should be next to the 'zero' mark on the scale. The other mark gives you the crater diameter to the nearest twenty miles.

Try measuring the distances across some of the huge deserts on the Moon.

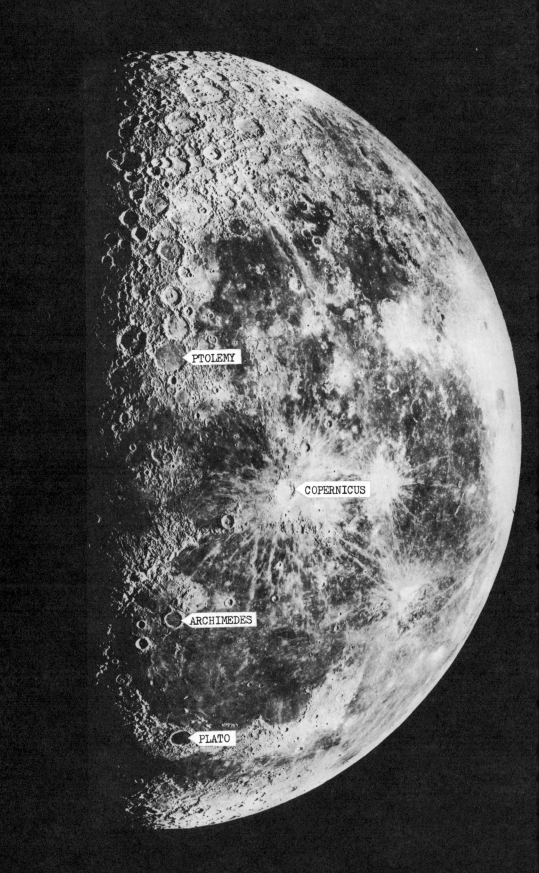

Here is a simple mathematical experiment which will tell us a surprising fact about measuring the edge or *circumference* of a circle.

Use a saucepan for your circle. Measure its *diameter* with a ruler.

Then wrap a piece of string round the saucepan to measure its circumference.

Simply make a pencil or crayon mark on both bits of string where they cross.

Then place the string against the edge of a ruler and measure the distance between the two marks you have made.

Now divide the diameter distance into the circumference.

Your answer will be approximately *three*.

To avoid annoying fractions make both your measurements in *eighths* of an inch. Remember:

Circumference ÷ Diameter = about three.

This is the pi sign - π

Do the experiment again, this time using a different size saucepan.

Again, divide the circumference by the diameter.

Your answer will still be exactly the same.

In fact *all* circles, whether huge like the Moon or tiny like a pinhole, have their circumferences about *three* times their diameters. This number is actually a little larger than three, if very accurate measurements are made. It has been carefully measured by mathematicians, who have found it to be 3.14 or $\frac{22}{7}$.

Mathematicians and scientists call this number Pi, using the Greek letter π, which corresponds to *our* P.

So to find the circumference of a circle, simply measure its diameter (which is quite simple and accurate) and *multiply the result by Pi!*

Actually 3.14 is not completely accurate. Modern mathematicians have found that it can be calculated to *many* places of decimals. Some have found it, using electronic brains, to as many as 700 places!

FOR EVERY CIRCLE IN THE UNIVERSE

DIAMETER TIMES π EQUALS CIRCUMFERENCE

CIRCUMFERENCE DIVIDED BY DIAMETER EQUALS π

OH YES? AND WHERE ARE ALL MY SAUCEPANS?

MUM! π = 3.1415 92653 58979 32384...

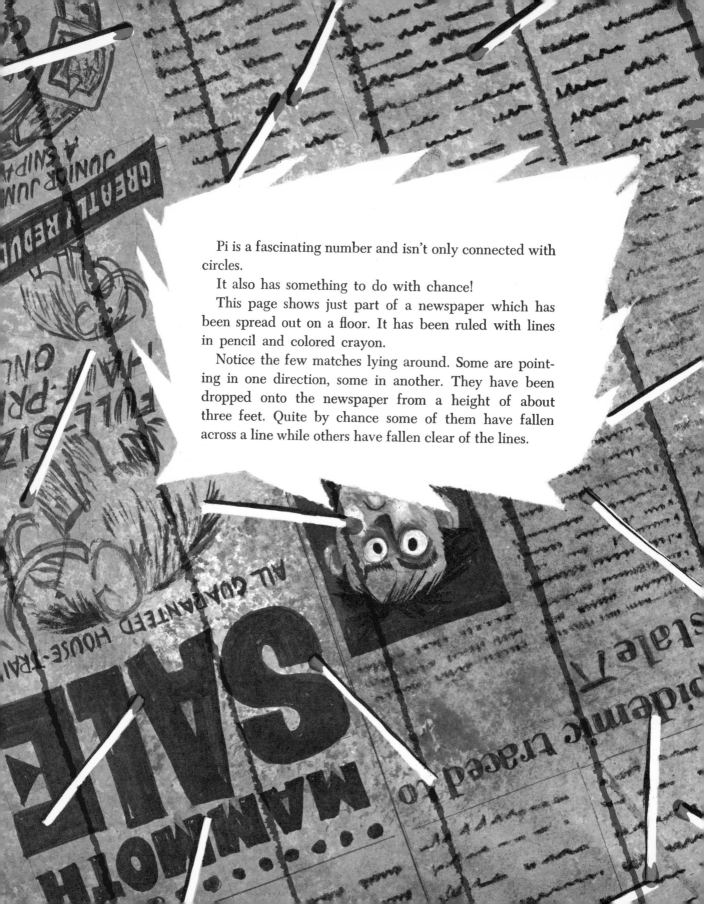

Pi is a fascinating number and isn't only connected with circles.

It also has something to do with chance!

This page shows just part of a newspaper which has been spread out on a floor. It has been ruled with lines in pencil and colored crayon.

Notice the few matches lying around. Some are pointing in one direction, some in another. They have been dropped onto the newspaper from a height of about three feet. Quite by chance some of them have fallen across a line while others have fallen clear of the lines.

But what has this got to do with Pi?

Try doing this match-dropping business yourself to find out.

Spread a newspaper double page out on the floor.

Rule lines across it. Make the spaces between lines the *same width as the length of a match*.

Now stand over the paper and drop or throw a handful of matches onto the paper. Don't try to aim them—just let them fall down anywhere.

Count all the matches which have fallen on the paper *across* a line.

Count all the matches which have fallen *clear* of the lines.

Pick up all the matches and do the same thing again. Now add up your totals.

Suppose altogether you've dropped 96 matches.

Then you will find that about 30 of them have fallen clear of the lines.

30 into 96 is a little over 3, or about Pi.

In fact if you keep dropping matches and keeping the score until you've dropped several hundred or more, you'll find that the number of "clear" matches will always divide into the total just over three, or exactly Pi times.

Things may be exactly the *same size* when we measure them with tapes or rulers, but may *look* as if they are different sizes.

In this drawing of an avenue of trees, everything in the distance looks smaller than the trees and the people near us.

This illusion is called *perspective*.

Even though they are all the same height, the trees far away look smaller than those close to us.

Here are some more odd illusions about size.

Which of these two 'schools' of fish swimming away from the whale's mouth is the longer?

Which is the *larger* circle, the white one or the black one?

Which of these two lines is longer?

The correct answers are on page 32.

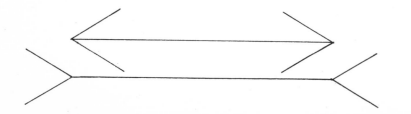

These two girls are twins, and believe it or not they are both the same height!

The room they are standing in has something wrong with it which makes one girl look like a giant and the other look like a dwarf.

What *is* wrong with the room? Turn to page 32 to find out.

But here's a clue. Read again about *perspective* on page 22!

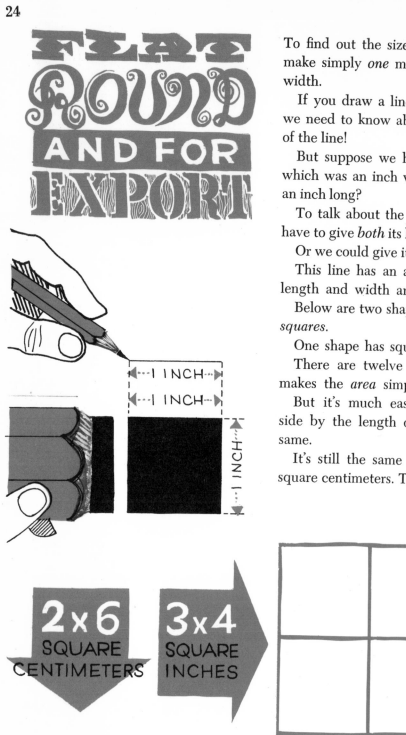

To find out the sizes of many things it's not enough to make simply *one* measurement, like length or height or width.

If you draw a line with a pencil, its *length* is all that we need to know about. The length is certainly the size of the line!

But suppose we had a line drawn with a pencil lead which was an inch wide? And we drew a "monster" line an inch long?

To talk about the size of this strange "line" we should have to give *both* its length *and* width.

Or we could give its *area*.

This line has an area of *one square inch*, because its length and width are one inch.

Below are two shapes which have been divided up into *squares*.

One shape has squares *one inch* by *one inch*.

There are twelve of these squares altogether, which makes the *area* simply twelve square inches.

But it's much easier to multiply the length of one side by the length of the other. The result is still the same.

It's still the same when we use a shape made up of square centimeters. The area is twelve square centimeters.

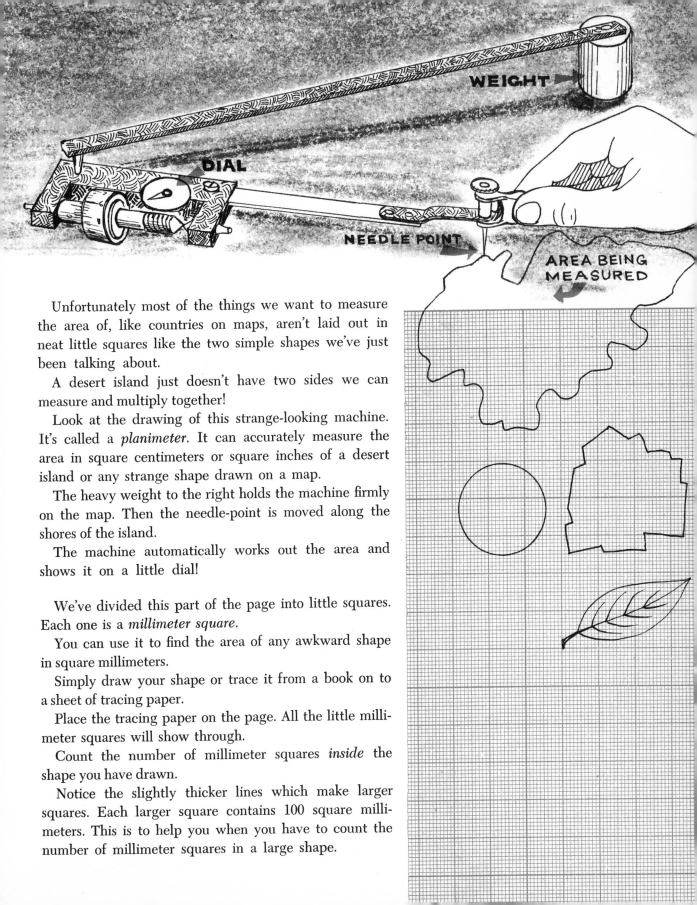

WEIGHT

DIAL

NEEDLE POINT

AREA BEING MEASURED

Unfortunately most of the things we want to measure the area of, like countries on maps, aren't laid out in neat little squares like the two simple shapes we've just been talking about.

A desert island just doesn't have two sides we can measure and multiply together!

Look at the drawing of this strange-looking machine. It's called a *planimeter*. It can accurately measure the area in square centimeters or square inches of a desert island or any strange shape drawn on a map.

The heavy weight to the right holds the machine firmly on the map. Then the needle-point is moved along the shores of the island.

The machine automatically works out the area and shows it on a little dial!

We've divided this part of the page into little squares. Each one is a *millimeter square*.

You can use it to find the area of any awkward shape in square millimeters.

Simply draw your shape or trace it from a book on to a sheet of tracing paper.

Place the tracing paper on the page. All the little millimeter squares will show through.

Count the number of millimeter squares *inside* the shape you have drawn.

Notice the slightly thicker lines which make larger squares. Each larger square contains 100 square millimeters. This is to help you when you have to count the number of millimeter squares in a large shape.

The pictures on these two pages show why mapmakers have a lot of trouble with the areas of countries and oceans of the world.

Imagine the world cut up into segments like an orange!

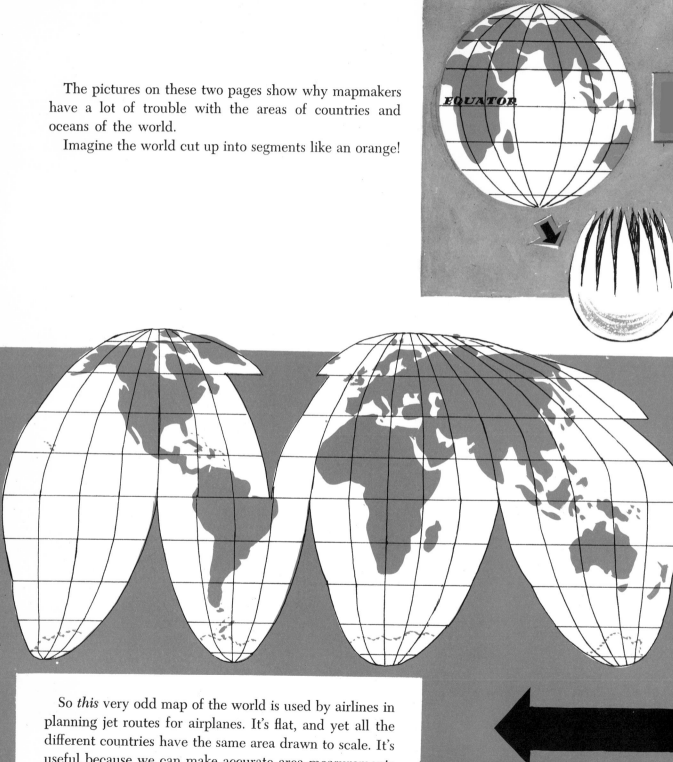

So *this* very odd map of the world is used by airlines in planning jet routes for airplanes. It's flat, and yet all the different countries have the same area drawn to scale. It's useful because we can make accurate area measurements anywhere on it.

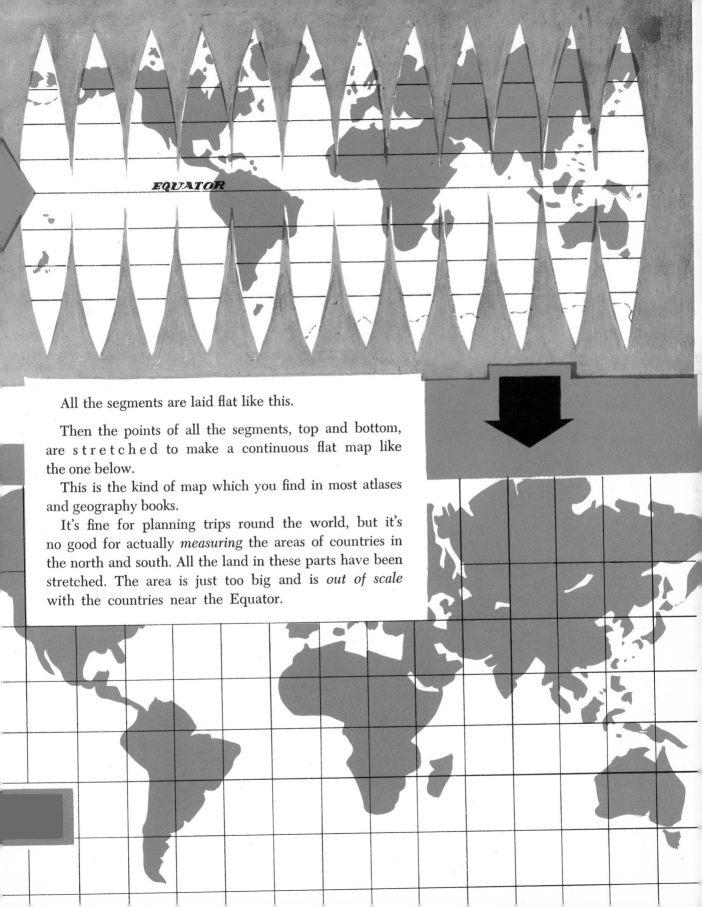

EQUATOR

All the segments are laid flat like this.

Then the points of all the segments, top and bottom, are s t r e t c h e d to make a continuous flat map like the one below.

This is the kind of map which you find in most atlases and geography books.

It's fine for planning trips round the world, but it's no good for actually *measuring* the areas of countries in the north and south. All the land in these parts have been stretched. The area is just too big and is *out of scale* with the countries near the Equator.

The *area* of a shape or an island is just a clever way of using *one* number for a number of measurements.

The *volume* of something can do the same thing.

A *cube* that is one foot high, one foot wide and one foot long has a volume of *one cubic foot*.

The big packing case ready for export is three feet high, three feet long and two feet wide.

We can't add a lot of cubes together to find its volume, because we can't see any. But we can do what we did with our shapes a few pages ago. Multiply all our measurements.

$3\times3\times2=18$

The packing case has a volume of eighteen cubic feet.

That's the surprising thing about volume, the fact that we get such a big number when we multiply all our small dimensions together.

Measure the height, width and length of your TV set *in inches*.

Multiply your measurements.

You never would have thought that a TV set could possibly contain so many cubic inches!

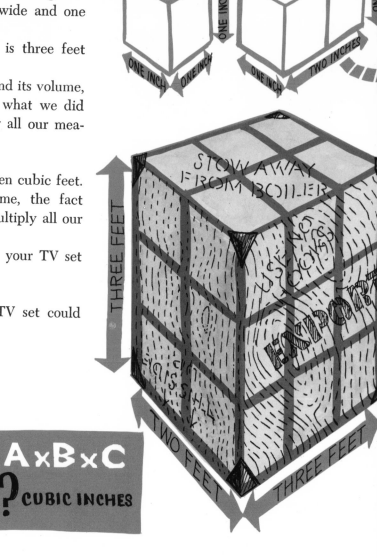

A x B x C
? CUBIC INCHES

If you know the area on which a square shape sits, you can find the volume quickly by multiplying the area by the *height*. The higher it is the greater its volume.

Volume is an area being "pulled up" straight by a balloon. The higher the balloon goes the bigger the volume gets.

1 x 1 x 1
ONE CUBIC INCH

1 x 2 x 1
TWO CUBIC INCHES

2 x 3 x 3
EIGHTEEN
CUBIC FEET

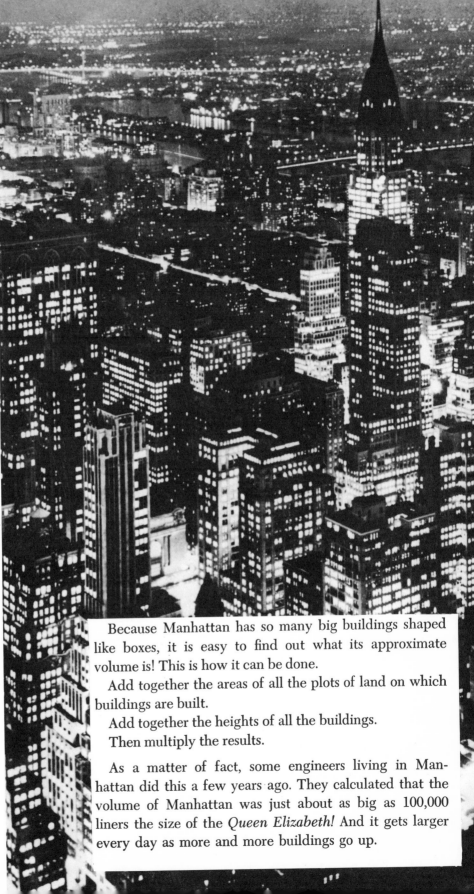

Because Manhattan has so many big buildings shaped like boxes, it is easy to find out what its approximate volume is! This is how it can be done.

Add together the areas of all the plots of land on which buildings are built.

Add together the heights of all the buildings.

Then multiply the results.

As a matter of fact, some engineers living in Manhattan did this a few years ago. They calculated that the volume of Manhattan was just about as big as 100,000 liners the size of the *Queen Elizabeth!* And it gets larger every day as more and more buildings go up.

PICTURE PUZZLE

Here is a picture puzzle about size and measuring. Two of the questions have a catch in them!

The correct solutions are printed *upside down* on the next page.

Which of these things would you expect to be measured in meters?

Which of these things is measured as a circumference?

Which of these things has its width measured simply as a letter of the alphabet?

Which of these things is used to measure *outside* something?

Which part of one of these things must *always* have the same size?

Which of these things has *area* but is only measured in length?

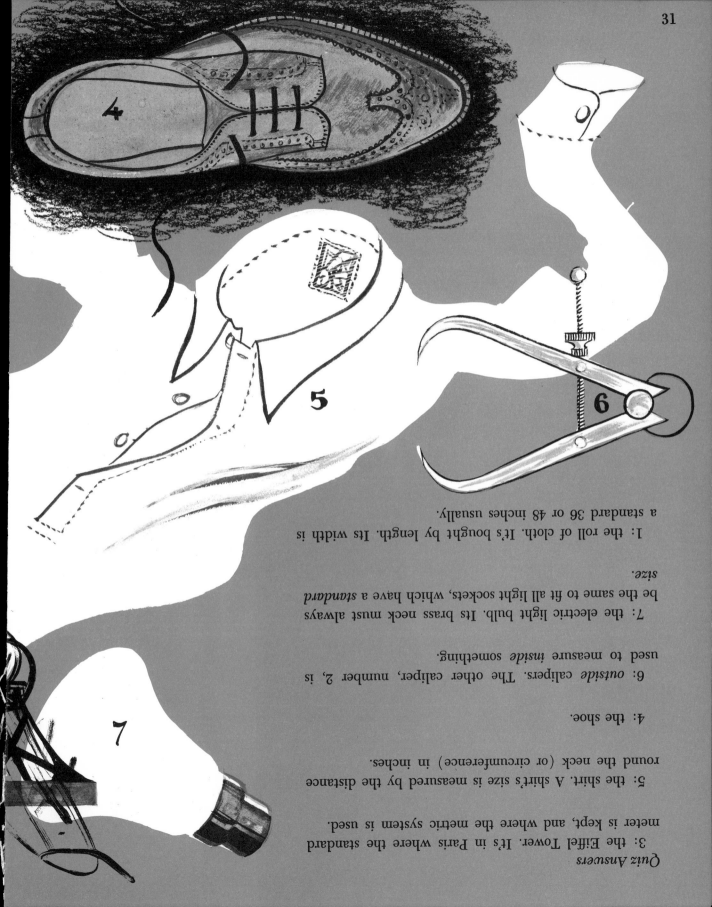

Quiz Answers

3: the Eiffel Tower. It's in Paris where the standard meter is kept, and where the metric system is used.

5: the shirt. A shirt's size is measured by the distance round the neck (or circumference) in inches.

4: the shoe.

6: *outside* calipers. The other caliper, number 2, is used to measure *inside* something.

7: the electric light bulb. Its brass neck must always be the same to fit all light sockets, which have a *standard size.*

1: the roll of cloth. It's bought by length. Its width is a standard 36 or 48 inches usually.

32

INDEX

Answers to illusions on page 22.

Both schools of fish are the same length.

The two lines are the same length. The lower one looks longer because of the extra short lines jutting out from it.

The white circle is the same size as the black one. The white expanse round the black circle takes away our attention and we think the circle is smaller than it is. The white circle, however, merely looks bigger because it is brighter!

It hardly looks it, but this room has been specially built to show a completely false perspective. The back wall slants backward from right to left. The ceiling near the left-hand corner is twice as high as it is at right. The left-hand girl is really much farther away. And, more curious still, the two windows are *not* the same size!

J E   171726
389
H28 Hatcher
        What size is it?

Date